Contents

Main: Spring-flowering candelabra primulas (*Primula pulverulenta*) beside Benmore Pond.

Foreword

It is a great personal pleasure to welcome you to Benmore Botanic Garden, a beautiful and very special place to visit from spring to autumn. The Garden is set in Loch Lomond & The Trossachs National Park – the wild landscape of the Cowal Peninsula, with its lochs and mountains, might seem an unlikely place to find a botanic garden. But the west of Scotland has a special climate with abundant rainfall, making it a perfect place to grow plants from mountains and temperate rainforests around the world.

Benmore is one of the four sites across which the Royal Botanic Garden Edinburgh distributes its precious living collections: plants that are samples of the world's natural heritage. If we are to succeed in protecting and conserving plants so that they can be restored to the wild these collections form a vital resource for the future. Whilst Benmore is one part of a national institution it is also utterly distinctive! Approaching the Redwood Avenue across the River Eachaig presents a garden entrance unrivalled in its majesty and drama by any I have seen. For me, this vista is a living symbol of the mindset of the gardener: a person who thinks long term, shaping their patch of the Earth according to a vision that expresses both their deep connection with the place and their determination to leave it better than they found it.

Beyond the Redwood Avenue there are formal garden landscapes comparable with other botanic gardens, but deeper still in Benmore lie a series of unusual and distinctive geographic plantings. Today, it is difficult to imagine what a remarkable experience walking through the Chilean Rainforest Glade will be when the hundreds of monkey puzzle trees have reached maturity. The giant redwoods will have added a few more metres and with our care and your support Benmore Botanic Garden will continue to flourish as a haven for some of the world's rarest and most valuable plants.

Stephen Blackmore FRSE
Regius Keeper
Royal Botanic Garden Edinburgh

Main: The many layers of Benmore Botanic Garden. Scottish ferns over look the specialist collection inside the newly restored Victorian Fernery, while the tall spires of conifers from around the world point to the plantations on the surrounding hillsides.

Curator's welcome

I always feel that Benmore is two gardens. It is rightly known for its fine collections of rhododendrons and conifers grown to immense stature in a dramatic mountain landscape.

We have developed this existing collection but at the same time created new landscapes with newly collected plants that are threatened in their natural habitat.

Benmore has enough space to grow whole groups of plants together. This creates a more natural-looking environment and allows the opportunity to hold greater genetic diversity, which is essential for a conservation collection.

In my 15 years as Curator, I have explored spectacular mountain landscapes, collecting plants to recreate aspects of Tasmania, Chile and Japan. Benmore is a large garden, but when you're travelling up to the tree line of the Chilean Andes, you realise the scale of what we are recreating.

Expeditions in recent years have taken me to California, in search of coastal redwoods and sugar pines as well as other conifers, rhododendrons and ferns. It was brilliant to see the giant redwoods there – at almost 150 years old Benmore's redwoods are impressive, but those I saw in California are on another scale, over 1,000 years old. No matter how prepared you are, it's hard to believe a tree can be that size!

Back at Benmore, in order for the collection to be looked after and further developed, our staff have to be highly skilled in the use of tools and equipment, capable of handling different tasks in all weathers and receptive to each other's ideas.

As a visitor, you will find that you can't do the Garden justice in one day. I hope you enjoy Benmore Botanic Garden with all it has to offer and have the opportunity to make many return visits, to explore further and discover more and perhaps become a Member.

Peter Baxter

Peter Baxter
Curator, Benmore Botanic Garden

Main: Overlooking the River Eachaig as it winds through Benmore estate beneath the wooded slopes of A'Chruach (or Benmore Hill), this dramatic photograph by Robert Moyes Adam, a member of RBGE staff, was taken in 1930 from Beinn Ruadh. Courtesy of St Andrews University Special Collections. RMA-H2373

Benmore Estate – a short planting history

The wild landscape of Benmore has always attracted adventurers and explorers. These ancient hunting grounds of the Dukes of Argyll became a romantic playground for 19th-century merchant princes: industrialists and businessmen with imagination, energy and money to spend on grand buildings and bold plantations within easy reach of the Clyde.

Bare hillside provided a blank canvas. The native cover of oak, birch and alder had given way to moorland as sheep arrived in the 18th century and this part of the Cowal Peninsula became known as the Vale of the Fleeces. By the early 19th century newly planted conifers were beginning to define the boundaries of Benmore as the estate grew along the River Eachaig valley between Holy Loch and Loch Eck.

Exploring the Garden today you find a trail left by a succession of different owners. Some of them stayed only a short time but by planting trees they were to make a mark on the landscape that may last for hundreds, even thousands, of years.

Not much is known about one of the earliest owners, Ross Wilson, beyond the fact that he planted the first conifers at Benmore in the 1820s. You will find some survivors, the oldest Scots pines, growing in the Garden among exotic newcomers in the Glen Massan Arboretum.

To get there you walk up the famous Redwood Avenue. The man who planted it was a wealthy American, Piers Patrick, possibly a tobacco baron, who bought Benmore in 1861 and sold it just nine years later. During that time he

A man of parts

James Duncan (1834–1905) was a chemist, philanthropist and entrepreneur who built a highly successful sugar-refining business. He was also an art lover with a passion for French paintings. In 1879 he built his picture gallery at Benmore to house over 300 paintings and opened it to the public in 1881.

Works by Delacroix, Rubens, Raeburn and Goya arrived by steamer at Dunoon to decorate what was described in 1885 as "one of the finest galleries in Europe … filled with choicest works of ancient and modern art".*

The fame was shortlived. When sugar prices dropped, Duncan had to sell his paintings – and Benmore. His collection is dispersed through galleries across the world and his prized Delacroix, *The Death of Sardanapalus*, hangs in the Louvre in Paris.

*From 'James Duncan of Benmore: a Remarkable Victorian Collector' Andrew Watson, *Journal of the Scottish Society for Art History Vol 14.*

built the tower and the courtyard and extended the estate along Loch Eck. In 1863 Patrick took the gamble of planting an avenue of giant redwoods (*Sequoiadendron giganteum*), grown from seed newly arrived from the west coast of North America. Had he any idea how well his 50 young redwoods would grow?

Perhaps Patrick's fortunes changed; at any rate in 1870 he sold the estate to a sugar refiner from Greenock. James Duncan was a wealthy industrialist (by then based in London) who literally transformed the landscape, planting over six million conifers and adding enormous glasshouses to the garden and a heated fernery to the hillside. At the same time he built an internationally

Above: The Redwood Avenue in the early 1900s interplanted with noble fir, since removed, around 40 years old and already casting long shadows. Courtesy of David Younger.

Left: James Duncan, c. 1900–1905. Permission of Principal and Fellows of Mansfield College, Oxford.

admired collection of art and a huge picture gallery to display it on the side of Benmore House. His fortune did not last long. When sugar prices collapsed, Duncan had to sell his paintings and then the estate to stave off bankruptcy.

The new owner was Henry J. Younger, the Edinburgh brewer, who bought Benmore in 1889 and demolished the picture gallery less than a year later. Although Younger had almost certainly bought the estate for hunting, shooting and fishing, he soon became interested in planting trees. His son Harry George Younger carried on planting when he inherited the estate in 1913, adding western red cedar (*Thuja plicata*) and larch (*Larix* x *eurolepis*), exotic flowering shrubs and the first of the rhododendrons near the house. In a golden Edwardian era, peacocks roamed the grounds, Harry Lauder entertained house guests at musical evenings (the music hall star owned

James Duncan commissioned a Berlin firm to make the ornamental iron gates at the Glen Massan entrance. The gates, said to have been designed for the 1878 Exposition Universelle in Paris, have been temporarily removed for restoration.

nearby Glenbranter estate) and a staff of 40 looked after woods and garden.

Times change but the trees go on growing. James Duncan's conifers form the backbone of today's Garden. In Piers Patrick's avenue, 49 of the 50 giant redwoods are still thriving –

standing 50 metres high they could grow twice as tall and last 2,000 years.

Harry George Younger's greatest legacy is the Garden itself. In 1924 he began negotiations to give Benmore to the nation, opening an opportunity to bring new colour and drama to the mountain.

Top left: An Edwardian afternoon on the steps in front of Benmore House – H. J. Younger stands in the pale top hat with son H. G. Younger in the peaked hat seated on his right.

Above: Initials of James Duncan inscribed in the gilded wrought iron of the Golden Gates.

Below: Benmore House with Duncan's picture gallery to the right and bronze stags in the foreground.

(Main Benmore images courtesy of David Younger)

Almost a hundred years ago, Sir Isaac Bayley Balfour, Regius Keeper of the Royal Botanic Garden Edinburgh, was urgently looking for space to grow the huge influx of plants from China brought back by Scotland's famous plant hunter George Forrest. RBGE was already moving young rhododendrons to a Forestry Commission site in Glenbranter, north of Benmore, when Harry George Younger made his better offer.

Benmore was closer to Dunoon ferries, it had a ready-made garden sheltered by mature trees and (like Glenbranter) a mild, moist climate more welcoming to Himalayan plants than drier, colder Edinburgh. In 1925, three years after Bayley Balfour's death, the rhododendrons were transferred from Glenbranter to Benmore, and in 1929 the Younger Botanic Garden became RBGE's first regional garden.

The Forestry Commission had overall care of the estate and ran forestry courses from Benmore House, while RBGE took responsibility for the garden and arboretum. During the first ten years, thousands of newly propagated plants, including many rhododendrons, were sent from Edinburgh to grow beneath the canopy of James Duncan's conifers.

Problems grew too. During the staff shortages of the Second World War, *Rhododendron ponticum* – the invasive pink-flowered alien planted as game cover by Duncan – began to dominate the hillside. By the late 1950s thickly planted Victorian trees allowed little room for new plants.

Younger Botanic Garden

It was to be "a wild and woodland garden on a magnificent scale . . . with a canopy of trees for plants from all parts of the world". With hindsight Harry George Younger's vision has a prophetic ring. The sanctuary of a woodland garden for the world's plants would become increasingly important by the end of the 20th century.

Right: Forrest's legacy, a blaze of spring colour on the hillside.

Below: George Forrest on expedition in China. His discoveries were to change the face of Scotland's gardens and establish RBGE's international reputation for research on temperate rhododendrons. By the time he died in 1932 he had introduced hundreds of new plants to cultivation. Many of his original introductions are now mature rhododendrons at Benmore.

When change came it was sudden and violent. Scotland's 1968 hurricane ripped out more than 500 trees over 40 m high, some more than 2.5 m wide. (The redwoods stood firm: of the original fifty only one, the weakest specimen, blew down.) By 1974, when RBGE took ownership of the 110 acre (44 ha) woodland garden and arboretum, the opportunity of new space was combined with a new sense of urgency.

With plants increasingly threatened in the wild – and growing awareness of climate change – once again the slopes of Benmore fired the imagination. Here was a chance to create a conservation project on a grand new scale. A bold experiment began in the 1980s, exploiting the Benmore climate to mimic temperate rainforest regions across the world. First came the Tasmanian Ridge above the old Fernery. The Bhutanese Glade followed after plant-collecting expeditions to Bhutan in the 1980s. And Chile arrived at the wildest and most westerly end of the Garden in 1996 after expeditions to collect wild seed from mountainous regions threatened by logging and fires.

Japan is the latest addition. By 2010 the dramatic Japanese Valley was emerging beside the Tasmanian Ridge, near the now restored Fernery. Expeditions to Japan provided seed for new colour on the slopes above Glen Massan, with maples and rhododendrons growing with the Japanese cedars planted 30 years earlier.

This is indeed "wild and woodland gardening on a magnificent scale" and it is a long process. You need patience and imagination to picture Tasmania, Bhutan, Japan and Chile 30 (or 300) years from now. Today Curator Peter Baxter and his small team of Garden staff are managing a project which stretches far into the future: as bold, visionary and optimistic as the planting of the Redwood Avenue 150 years ago.

Puck's Hut

On a sunny September day in 1928 crowds arrived by steamer and charabanc to see the building designed by Sir Robert Lorimer in memory of The King's Botanist of Scotland.

The Isaac Bayley Balfour Memorial was erected in a woodland ravine by the Forestry Commission in tribute to the man who first thought of creating a west coast botanic garden.

Known as 'Puck's Hut', it was tiled in western red cedar and panelled with wood representing the varied timbers of Benmore.

Benmore also remembers William Wright Smith, Bayley Balfour's successor, who brought the vision to life, transferring thousands of George Forrest's rhododendrons from Edinburgh to Benmore. Sir William's memorial stands by the Viewpoint. Puck's Hut now sits at the top of the Formal Garden.

The Younger (Benmore) Trust

The Younger family retains a lasting link with Benmore through a trust set up by Harry George Younger in 1928 to help maintain the "amenity, utility and beauty" of the policies and gardens.

The Younger (Benmore) Trust has enabled staff to go on plant-collecting expeditions to Bhutan, Japan and Chile as well as supporting major projects in the Garden.

Practical gifts include donations towards converting the old sawmill to the Courtyard Gallery, building the Viewpoint shelter, buying the Benmore Explorer and towards restoring the Fernery.

Above: Puck's Hut, framed by tips of *Pinus mugo* 'Gnom' in the shelter of the Formal Garden.
Left: Inside the Hut a memorial plaque pays tribute to the 19th-century plantings of James Duncan.

REMEMBER·JAMES·DUNCAN·WHO
HAD·THE·FORESIGHT·AND·COURAGE
TO·ORIGINATE·THE·PLANTING·WHICH
CLOTHED·THESE·HILLS·AND·GLENS
WITH·THE·WOODS·YOU·NOW·ENJOY

Below: The armillary sphere in the Formal Garden commemorates Harold Fletcher, Regius Keeper from 1956–1970 (growing nearby is *Rhododendron fletcherianum*).

TIMELINE

1820	Ross Wilson plants Scots pine and other conifers at Benmore (first on Cowal Peninsula)
1863	Piers Patrick plants Redwood Avenue along the driveway to Benmore House
1870–1889	James Duncan transforms the landscape, planting 6.5 million trees and adding glasshouses to the Formal Garden and a heated Fernery on the hillside **A**
1890s	Henry James Younger continues planting conifers **B**
1913	Harry George Younger inherits the estate and experiments with new plantings of Japanese larch and western red cedar
1929	Harry George Younger gifts Benmore to the nation via the Forestry Commission. Royal Botanic Garden Edinburgh has responsibility for managing the garden and arboretum
1930s	Many conifers and rhododendrons are transferred from Edinburgh to Benmore **C**
1950s	Reclaiming the garden after neglect during the war years and the invasion of *Rhododendron ponticum*
1968	Hurricane fells 500 mature trees; four years of clearing opens the way to new planting
1974	Ownership transfers from Forestry Commission to RBGE
1987	Tasmanian Ridge is planted above Fernery ruins **D**
1989	Bhutanese Glade is planted after expedition to Bhutan
1994–1997	Clearing hillside and planting Chilean Rainforest Glade after expeditions to Chile
1999	Younger Botanic Garden officially renamed as Benmore Botanic Garden (with the blessing of David Younger)
2000	Courtyard Gallery opens in converted sawmill
2002	Benmore becomes part of the Loch Lomond & The Trossachs National Park
2007	Planting the Japanese Valley
2009	Fernery reopens **E**

A

B

C

D

E

A botanic garden in the National Park

In a way Benmore is much larger than life: a make-believe mountain landscape shaped and coloured with giant conifers and huge-leaved rhododendron trees from the other side of the world. But it's the home-grown touches – branches silvered with lichen, ground covered with bright green moss – that add the magic.

Nature infiltrates the man-made design and that is what makes Benmore a perfect gateway to Scotland's first national park. The Garden has been part of the Argyll Forest Park since it was established by the Forestry Commission in 1935 as Britain's first public forest park. Now Benmore is

Above: Nature adds an elfin touch to Benmore trees.

Below: As a gateway to the National Park, Benmore offers a glimpse of the surrounding landscape in microcosm (with the added benefit of plant labels).

at the south-westerly tip of Loch Lomond & The Trossachs National Park, which opened in 2002.

The National Park covers some of the most spectacularly beautiful scenery in Scotland with around 720 square miles (1,865 sq km) of moors, mountains, rivers, lochs and glens.

Yet for all its dramatic grandeur none of this is wilderness and not much of it is truly natural.

Just like Benmore, the landscape in the Park is the result of people's

actions and nature's reactions. Highland scenery is a product of human economic ventures of the past (like tanning and making gunpowder) and present (fishing, farming and forestry). Grazing animals helped to turn woodland into moorland of rough grass and bracken. Trees have been felled and planted according to changing events downriver or overseas.

Stretching from Dunoon to Tyndrum in Perthshire, the National

Water runs through the National Park.
Right: Benmore's stretch of the River Massan.
Below left: Tarbet Pier on Loch Lomond.
Below right: A rocky outcrop of the River Massan at the southern boundary, outside the Garden.

Park gives new purpose to an area rich in human and natural history, restoring native habitat for wildlife, encouraging a sustainable economy and offering people reasons to return to live and work in rural communities.

From the beginning, Curator Peter Baxter saw a role for the only botanic garden in the Park: welcoming and introducing visitors to an extraordinary environment. The Garden's 120 acres (49 ha) of carefully managed ground is in effect a microcosm of the Argyll landscape – mountains, valleys, rivers and rocks – planted with trees.

Outside Benmore the hills are covered with commercial forests, fast-growing exotic conifers many of which are from the Pacific coast of North America. Inside the Garden you can see how some of these same trees look when they are allowed to grow old. And there are glimpses of other mountain regions. You can climb a hill in Bhutan and explore a Japanese valley with the luxury of labels to tell you names of plants and discreet panels explaining why they are here. Many of them are threatened in their native habitat. But you can also get a feeling of the native oak woodland of Scotland's west coast. Temperate rainforest dripping with lichens and moss demonstrate a rich habitat which is also a priority for conservation.

Each Benmore planting has a story to tell. As in the wider National Park, conservation demands a sensitive balancing act, knowing when to intervene – removing invasive species like *Rhododendron ponticum* which choke the growth of native plants and destroy wildlife habitats – and when to leave nature well alone. In the famously mild and moist climate every surface – each rock, log and tree trunk – can become an ecosystem rich in lichens, liverworts and mosses of all kinds. In a garden of giants, these tiny touches of fairyland are the real Scotland.

The Garden setting

Mountains set the scene and bring the rain, creating a unique atmosphere that feels much more than an hour's journey from Glasgow – and further than just seven miles from Dunoon.

Main: Looking down over the Formal Garden from Benmore's western slopes. Rhododendrons and conifers flourish in Benmore's climate, with its mild temperatures and frequent rainfall.

Surrounded by steep mountains, the 120-acre (49-ha) Garden begins in the valley of the River Eachaig between Holy Loch and Loch Eck, then climbs the lower slopes of A'Chruach (locally called Benmore) to a viewpoint 137 m (450 ft) above sea level. From here, unless mist is lying low, you can see Holy Loch and bare tops of neighbouring mountains.

Climate

Even on dry days clouds may cling to the mountain tops. When air meets mountains it is forced to rise, water vapour turns into clouds and eventually falls as rain or snow. In the microclimate of the Garden you might find rain even when Dunoon is dry.

Benmore can be described as temperate rainforest because the rainfall is so heavy and it falls so often. The wettest of the four RBGE Gardens, it receives an average of 2,569 mm (102 inches) a year – more than three times as much as Edinburgh.

The wettest year on record was 1948 with 3,365 mm (132 inches); 2009 was the 10th wettest year at Benmore since records began in 1931, with a total rainfall of 2,844 mm (112 inches).

Colder than Logan Botanic Garden, which enjoys the full benefit of the Gulf Stream, Benmore is not free of frost for long – in 2009 there were around 99 frost-free days between spring and autumn. But tree cover provides a stable climate of cool summers and relatively mild winters for a huge range of plants from mountainous regions across the world.

Benmore and Edinburgh rainfall statistics
10-year averages in mm

Garden	Jan	Feb	Mar	Apr	May	Jun	July	Aug	Sept	Oct	Nov	Dec	Total
Edinburgh	72.6	49.6	47.9	43.7	47.4	60.0	70.1	87.9	57.0	88.0	64.6	52.3	741.1
Benmore	351.7	212.7	234.1	142.3	145.4	151.6	129.6	201.8	206.9	273.8	291.9	254.3	2,596.2

Geology and soils

Touch the rocks at Benmore and you are in contact with Precambrian times, 500–700 million years ago, when there was no Atlantic Ocean and Scotland was joined to the North American continent.

Like much of the Scottish Highlands, the Garden rests on mica-schist rock, formed by 'mountain building' forces of intense heat and compression as continents collided. Today, layers of rock glitter with metallic flecks of mica. In places the surface erodes to offer fertile niches for ferns and mosses as you can see in the almost vertical rock face in Glen Massan.

Lush growth conceals surprisingly thin topsoil – where mature trees have fallen you can see just how thin it is. Peaty humus on high ground gives way to sandier loam near the Pond. In general the highly acidic ground is ideal for conifers and rhododendrons and Scottish native plants claiming the ground beneath them.

A riot of rhododendrons

It begins as early as February. When the Garden is quiet and most plants subdued, the first tight buds open and the early rhododendrons flower defiantly in the cold winter wind. *Rhododendron barbatum* is among the first, with large pompoms in startling red. The tree-sized *R. arboreum* brings bursts of vivid pinks. By March, when the Garden opens to the public, more rhododendrons may already be in bloom.

With more than 3,000 plants of around 300 species, arranged by botanical grouping or geographic origin, Benmore has been described as a "living textbook of the genus *Rhododendron*". But in the flowering season it feels more like a party – a celebration in which this flamboyant plant group bloom in succession, showing off their most decadent colours and delicate scents. In April and May, the party reaches its peak and the slopes of Benmore are alive with brilliant reds, rich purples, shocking pinks and papery whites.

While the flowers are dazzling, there is much more to rhododendrons than extravagant blossom. The flowering season for each species can be short and intense, but the interest continues year round with striking bark and varied foliage. *R. barbatum* has plum-coloured peeling bark and bristly hairs on the stalks of its leaves. The large-leaved rhododendrons, such as those of subsection Grande, have huge, glossy, dark green leaves. *R. schilppenbachii* brings surprise autumn colour when its whorls of spoon-shaped leaves turn to rich yellow and red.

Rhododendrons are an integral part of Benmore's history – the main reason for RBGE needing a west coast garden. In the early 20th century, plant collectors such as George Forrest, Ernest Wilson and Joseph Rock brought back hundreds of new plants to Britain, including many new species of rhododendron. RBGE needed somewhere with enough space and the right conditions to grow these plants, and with its mild climate, high

Left: Benmore is renowned for its extensive collection of rhododendrons, which bring a dazzle of colour through spring and early summer.

Insets left to right: *Rhododendron atlanticum* and *R. cinnabarinum*.

Fleeing for his life from an attack on a missionary community on his first visit to China in 1905, George Forrest (1873–1932) still took notes of the plants as he travelled, rifle in hand, through snow and ice in the high mountains. Undaunted, he returned six times between 1910 and 1930 to the mountains he described as the "flower garden of the world". He was particularly enchanted by the sight of rhododendrons in their native habitat, the huge canopies forming bands of bright colour on the slopes of the mountains. Forrest brought back thousands of plants, including more than 300 species of rhododendron. These collections transformed British gardens and shaped the future direction of RBGE's research. Pressed specimens of all the plants he collected were sent for identification in RBGE's Herbarium, where he had worked before his travels.

rainfall and acidic soil, Benmore offered the perfect habitat. In the 1920s and 1930s, hundreds of rhododendrons were grown in the Edinburgh Nursery and then transferred to the wild, wet mountainside in Argyll.

The collections flourished in their new home. Many specimens grown from seed gathered by the early plant hunters can be seen in the Garden today. With room to spread, the older rhododendrons have achieved a true wild beauty not usually possible in cultivation. The scale and stature of the plants stops you in your tracks as you walk through the Garden. Looking up into the canopy behind Benmore House, you can feel a sense of the dramatic colour of the forests on the lower slopes of the Himalayas.

Old stories mingle with new. One of the favourites at Benmore is a mighty *R. sinogrande*, a "magnificent species" discovered by Forrest in China in 1912. It has grown to a stately size, its canopy flowing with huge trusses of creamy-yellow flowers in April. Among the new arrivals at Benmore are 28 young plants of *R. sinogrande*, collected from the Gaoligong Shan mountains on the border of China and Burma. Now very rare in the wild, these plants will be part of a conservation collection, as well as forming the Garden of the future – it will be at least 15 years before they flower.

Top: *Rhododendron semnoides* flourishes in the shelter of this wooded garden, bearing trusses of pinky-white flowers in April.

Giants of Benmore

Old trees keep us in touch with our human past. They have stories to tell about the people who found, felled or planted them, and the browsing animals that shape or stunt their growth. The oldest become ecosystems of their own: bustling communities of interconnected living creatures of all shapes and sizes. Still under 200 years old, many of Benmore's greatest trees are only just beginning to tell their story.

Towering above us, the trees of Benmore are awe-inspiring not just because of their size but because they seem so old. The oldest have already outlived their human collectors and planters by generations. Yet – storms, pests, human behaviour and climate change permitting – they could last for centuries more. In the sanctuary of the Garden they have at least a fighting chance.

Main: Giant redwoods are the world's largest living trees (by volume) though not the tallest. That claim belongs to the coastal redwoods which also thrive at Benmore.

Coastal redwood

Even taller than giant redwoods in the wild, the world's tallest temperate tree is the coastal redwood, *Sequoia sempervirens*, native to a narrow coastal belt in California where some trees grow to more than 110 m in height. A specimen planted in 1872 at the time of James Duncan now stands 43.5 m high. In 2009 Curator Peter Baxter took part in a plant-collecting expedition across the Sierra Nevada in California, bringing new seed to increase the genetic diversity growing in the Garden.

Douglas fir ▲

Perhaps it is fitting that Benmore's tallest tree is a Douglas fir (*Pseudotsuga menziesii*), whose English and Latin names honour two famous Scottish explorers.

David Douglas saw the trees almost as soon as he set foot on the shores of the Columbia River on his first expedition up the wild west coast of North America in 1825. Following the trail of another remarkable Scottish plant collector, Douglas introduced seed from the trees first discovered by Archibald Menzies in 1793.

Many of Benmore's great conifers were introduced to Scotland by Douglas, providing the seeds for Scotland's forestry plantations. They also fired the imagination of landowners like James Duncan. This tree, planted in the 1870s, is 57m tall – you will find it in Glen Massan Arboretum between the foot of the Bhutanese Glade and Chilean Rainforest Glade.

Giant redwood

When the Redwood Avenue was planted in 1863 the American Civil War was at its height and Queen Victoria ruled the British Empire. Benmore's *Sequoiadendron giganteum* are now 50 m high but mere youngsters at 150 years old. The oldest known giant redwood reached 3,500 years (according to the ring count). Dinosaurs browsed their ancestors more than 65 million years ago.

In their native California, giant redwoods tend to grow in groves. Redwood avenues became a 19th-century status symbol after the trees were discovered high in the Sierra Nevada during the 1849 Gold Rush. Seed, introduced to Britain by the Cornish plant explorer William Lobb, produced young trees cleverly sold as Wellingtonias by Veitch nurseries (the Duke of Wellington died in 1852).

Benmore's avenue is not the oldest but it is the best in Britain. Racing skywards, the Garden trees grew rapidly while wild groves disappeared. Soft, spongy bark, which evolved to protect the species from fire, proved no match for the power saw. In California giant redwoods are now found only in protected national parks.

Southern beeches ▲

Conifers are not the only record-breakers in the Garden. The Chilean *Nothofagus betuloides* and New Zealand's black beech *Nothofagus solandri* are two of the largest in Britain.

◀ Monkey puzzles

The young trees on the slopes of A'Chruach have a long way to go but older specimens on the lawns of Benmore House and on the path near the entrance give an idea of the dramatic impact of a mature monkey puzzle forest. On the mountains of Chile these trees can grow to 50 m and over 1,000 years old.

Their Latin name *Araucaria araucana* refers to the native Araucanos people who harvested the seeds for food. Seeds – first brought back by Archibald Menzies in 1795 – soon produced distinctive spiky garden trees across Britain.

A national emblem of Chile, *A. araucana* is an endangered species protected by law. But outside the safety of the national parks, monkey puzzle trees are at risk from grazing, burning and clearing for commercial plantations.

Western hemlock ▼

The Garden's finest western hemlock (*Tsuga heterophylla*) is possibly the tallest specimen in Britain at over 51m. This one – to the west of Benmore House – was planted in the 1870s, roughly 50 years after David Douglas first saw hemlocks growing along the Pacific coast of North America.

From 1851 these conifers began to decorate British gardens and spread through commercial plantations. With its characteristic drooping leading shoot, western hemlock grows quickly and self-seeds so freely that it is one of the Garden's biggest weeds.

Interestingly, Benmore's giants have outgrown older specimens at Dawyck Botanic Garden. In the cold, dry Scottish Borders, a hemlock planted in 1860 is now 43 m – almost 10 m shorter than Benmore's younger tree growing on the hill above Benmore House.

Scots pine ▶

Not the biggest, but the oldest – Scots pines (*Pinus sylvestris*) have been growing in what is now called Golden Gates Avenue in the Glen Massan Arboretum since 1820, the year George IV became king of England and Scotland.

Spreading from the Arctic Circle to southern Spain, Scots pines are one of only three conifers (the others are yew and juniper) native to Scotland, where they occur naturally in the Highlands. They were deliberately introduced to the Cowal Peninsula by a pioneering planter, Ross Wilson, who changed the landscape with spruce, larch and these old Scots pines.

Scots pine is a 'keystone species', supporting a thriving ecosystem of plants, insects, birds and animals. The oldest recorded in Scotland is 520 years.

Conifer Conservation

Gardens can be a safe haven for the world's threatened trees. RBGE grows 69 per cent of the world's conifer species, and of the four Gardens Benmore can support the widest range. The International Conifer Conservation Programme (ICCP) was set up in 1991 to build on the huge wealth of knowledge and natural resources growing in the gardens of Britain and Ireland. Expeditions add new generations of young trees, building a store of genetic diversity for potential future restoration of forests in the wild.

This page: Felling a mature beech tree (*Fagus sylvatica*) which was in decline.
Right above and below: Tree-felling is winter work; even with heavy machinery clearing the timber can take several days.

These collections provide raw materials for RBGE's work in documenting and conserving plants, many of which are threatened in their natural habitat. The current plantings are shaped by RBGE's *Collections Policy*, which designates target species for each of the four Gardens, based on historic legacy and future conservation potential.

Benmore offers an ideal sanctuary for plants from the world's wild, wet mountain habitats. The sheer size allows for large-scale plantings, ensuring a broad genetic mix for conservation collections. It also makes for challenging gardening! Benmore's small team of horticultural staff have an awesome task to manage 49 hectares and more than 11,000 plants, in frequent wet weather on very steep slopes.

This is muscular gardening – scaling vast trees with chainsaws, moving huge boulders with tractors. It takes both brains and brawn to execute a garden design on this scale. Yet it also requires great sensitivity to nurture new plantings. All in all it's a mixture of trial and error, expertise and observation, physical exertion and patience. Above all, it's about vision.

Managing a mountainside garden

"All this beauty has a purpose," wrote Adrian Higgins in the *Washington Post* in February 2007, describing a visit to Benmore. It's a succinct summary of botanic gardens in the 21st century. The plantings are more than an aesthetically delightful display, more than a celebration of centuries of exploration and discovery in the plant kingdom. A new purpose has now evolved – these plantings make a vital contribution to the conservation of the world's plantlife.

In the good old days . . .

Many hands tackled the heavy
work. In the 19th century, James
Duncan employed gangs of workers
in a decade of intensive planting.
While a dozen men dug slits with
spades, teams of young boys and
girls inserted saplings – 4,000 trees
to the acre – hauled up steep slopes
by Shetland ponies and carts. In the
early 20th century, the Youngers ran
the estate with around 40 gardening
staff (plus foresters and ghillies),
using scythes and sickles to tame
the hillside.

In today's Garden . . .

There are more tractors than wheel-
barrows. Almost unbelievably a small
team of only 11 (at present) gardening
staff manage the challenging task
of gardening 49 hectares of planted
ground (much of it steep or near

vertical). Heavy machinery reduces
the need for man (and woman) power.
Strimmers and chainsaws replace
scythes and sickles and Garden staff
have certificates for aerial tree work,
in the use of chainsaws, wood chippers,
brush cutters, herbicide applicators –
and in First Aid.

Above: Felling a tree was an even more labour-
intensive job before the invention of power
tools. This photograph shows estate workers
clearing heavy timber in the days of the
Younger family. Courtesy of David Younger.

Right: A tractor helps to lift a rhododendron,
heavy root ball and all, for planting.

Taming the hillside

A new plantation might take 20 or 30 years to display its true potential but visions for the future start with hard work in the present – and a respectful eye on the past. There are set key steps to each development.

Even with power tools, felling a tree, cutting it up and winching out the timber can take several days.

Large trees are left or removed depending on their value, whether they block or frame a view and the role they might play in nursing new stock.

Drainage is essential at Benmore. Open ditches prevent heavy rain washing away young plants and eroding the hillside. Paths and bridges follow contours of the land, allowing Garden staff to reach plants and inviting visitors to explore.

Preparing ground for planting. Soil is analysed and compacted earth dug over. Even semi-mature plants can be moved using special lifting and planting gear.

Young trees and shrubs need protection. Wire cages keep out animal pests. Controlled spraying reduces competition from natural regeneration.

Nature soon takes over at Benmore as mosses, ferns and grasses colonise the ground floor.

Benmore in numbers

120 acres (**49** ha)
11 horticultural staff
5 tractors
12 Garden Guides
2,596 mm (**102** inches) average annual rainfall
15 km drains
11.8 km paths
80 benches
3,000 rhododendron plants (**300** species)
57 m tallest tree (Douglas fir)

Main: Lush tree ferns (*Dicksonia antartica*) dominate low-lying forests in the protection of Mount Field National Park in Tasmania.

Right: Peter Baxter meets a grass tree (*Xanthorrhoea australis*) during the RBGE expedition to Tasmania.

The Tasmanian Ridge began with a selection of endangered species found only on the large mountainous island to the south of mainland Australia. In the mid 1980s a steep and challenging slope above Benmore's then ruined Fernery was cleared and planted with young trees grown from seed collected by RBGE staff: Tasmanian cedars (*Athrotaxis laxifolia, A. cupressoides, A. selaginoides*), chestnut pine (*Diselma archeri*) and the extraordinary Huon pine (*Lagarostrobos franklinii*).

A path was cut into the ridge in 1994 and new seed collected in 1998, then in 2005 another RBGE expedition took the 10,800 mile trip 'down under'.

Tasmania is a sparsely peopled island; a plant explorer's paradise sheltering flora and fauna found nowhere else on the planet. The Tasmanian devil's blood-curdling screech echoes through tall eucalyptus; old growth forests dominated by gnarled southern beech shelter possums, tree frogs, tiger snakes and birds such as the olive whistler and green rosella. But, like every other biodiversity

The Tasmanian Ridge

As usual the trees came first. Seeds of ancient conifers collected on the island of Tasmania inspired Benmore's first attempt to recreate the look and feel of a landscape on the other side of the world.

From Mount Field National Park in Tasmania to Benmore Botanic Garden in Argyll – young specimens of *Eucalyptus regnans* made the long journey with the help of RBGE horticulturist Robert Unwin.

Robert, who works in the Edinburgh Garden, collected the seed from the forest floor beneath stands of mature *Eucalyptus regnans*, the Tasmanian oak or stringy gum, which is the world's tallest flowering tree, growing up to 100 m.

Back in Edinburgh, Robert regularly checked progress in the Nursery as the seed quickly germinated and young plants grew rapidly. A year later he completed the journey by helping to plant the trees on the Tasmanian Ridge at Benmore.

hotspot in the world, these unique ecosystems are threatened by human activities. The devil (a meat-eating marsupial) is endangered along with an extraordinary wealth of rainforest creatures. Outside Tasmania's national parks, ancient endemic trees are at risk from logging, mining and fire.

Guided by Tasmanian botanists and horticulturists, the RBGE team – Peter Baxter, Barry Unwin and Robert Unwin – explored the national parks, climbing through cool rainforest dripping with lichen to alpine tops covered with mounds of ground-hugging plants. On the way they

met some of Australia's oldest and tallest trees and one of the oldest living organisms on Earth: a huge Huon pine at least 10,000 but maybe up to 30,000 years old. This single tenacious male specimen has layered its way across Mount Read on the island's west coast. "Like a jungle of hundreds of trees tumbling down the hillside," as Robert Unwin described it.

Back at Benmore the Tasmanian Ridge has spread down the hillside to make room for young plants grown from seed collected on that expedition. While more tender specimens were dispersed to Logan Botanic Garden on the south-west coast of Scotland, the hardier trees, shrubs and herbaceous plants are settling into life on the Argyll hillside.

Steep slopes, thin soil and trespassing deer make it a challenging environment. The plants must go into the ground when they are small so they can develop strong root systems to anchor them securely against the wind. It will take time for the new southern beech, eucalyptus and tree ferns to evoke a Tasmanian landscape but there is still plenty to discover on the rugged hillside. Climbing the path above the Fernery you can get close to a display of rare flowering plants: crimson bottle brush callistemons, white eucryphias and the rare iris-like *Diplarrhena* which began life as tiny seeds on a moist stream bank half a world away.

Top: Path development on Benmore's Tasmanian Ridge.
Below left: *Eucryphia milliganii*.
Below right: Fern *Gleichenia*.

The Bhutanese Glade

Climbing up into the mountains of Bhutan, RBGE staff on a seed-collecting expedition in 1984 were struck by the layers of different habitats that they passed through. From lush, deciduous forests of the lowlands, they trekked through blue pines and enormous rhododendrons in the foothills, on through silver firs and hemlock and up to the alpine pasture of the high mountains.

The Kingdom of Bhutan lies in the eastern Himalayas, with the towering mountains of Tibet to the north and the Bengal plains of India along its southern border. The huge range of altitudes contributes to the astonishing richness of flora and fauna – in an area just over half the size of Scotland there are more than 5,500 species of plants (compared to Britain's 1,500 species). In recognition of this botanical wealth, Bhutan has been designated one of the world's ten hotspots for the conservation of plant biodiversity. And while much of the world is losing its biodiversity at an alarming rate, Bhutan has retained much of its pristine natural habitat, thanks to a governing philosophy which values the environment as an integral part of the nation's health, wealth and happiness.

Back in Scotland, expedition members were inspired to create a microcosm of the Bhutanese mountains on a south-facing slope in Benmore Botanic Garden. Planting the Bhutanese Glade began in 1989, using seed collected on the expeditions in Bhutan, and a second phase of planting

Clockwise from main: The misty mountains of Bhutan are recreated on the slopes of Benmore (**inset**); *Betula utilis*; *Rhododendron kesangiae*; teaching plant identification to young Bhutanese botanists using the *Flora of Bhutan*.

Gross National Happiness

Working in Bhutan was an inspirational experience for RBGE's scientists, horticulturists and education staff. Bhutan is the only Buddhist kingdom in the world and its people are custodians of a value system which acknowledges that happiness is dependent on the spiritual and emotional well-being of the people, through the preservation of culture and the natural environment. Celebrating the completion of the *Flora* in 2002, the then Bhutanese Minister for Agriculture Lyonpo Dr Kinzang Dorji explained how in Bhutan "Gross National Happiness is considered more important than the Gross Domestic Product. An increase in income and technology ... loses its meaning beyond a certain threshold when the increase in material consumption is not accompanied by a concomitant rise in happiness."

in 2001 added a new generation of trees and shrubs as well as herbaceous perennials on the woodland floor. Now visitors to Benmore can undertake their own expedition to Bhutan, experiencing the changing plantlife as they climb through five different vegetation zones. This wild and tranquil area of the Garden highlights Bhutan's flora, from rhododendrons, firs and birches to the juniper scrub of the high mountains. It also celebrates RBGE's ongoing relationship with this extraordinary kingdom.

RBGE has been working in partnership with Bhutan for more than 30 years. This began in 1978 with a lengthy collaboration to produce a complete *Flora of Bhutan* – an account of all the plants of the area. After twenty-five years and numerous field expeditions, the nine-volume work was completed. The project created lasting connections between RBGE staff and botanists in Bhutan and the *Flora* has become a valuable practical tool for Bhutanese foresters and naturalists.

Bhutanese government ministers visited RBGE to celebrate the completion of the *Flora* and began a new chapter in the partnership: the creation of a botanic garden in Serbithang, close to Bhutan's capital of Thimphu. The project was realised

through an ongoing exchange of staff and skills between RBGE and Serbithang. While Bhutanese botanists worked at Edinburgh's gardens, laboratories and Herbarium, RBGE staff were seconded to Bhutan to contribute to the development of the new garden – building infrastructure and designing planting schemes and education programmes.

As they worked together, the botanists from both countries also sowed the seeds for future collaboration. Current plans include a pictorial field guide to Bhutan's flowering plants and creating an online database. Future joint expeditions are also being planned, to further explore and study, understand and to

stock both the new botanic garden in Serbithang and the celebration of Bhutan on the slopes of Benmore.

Above: Chile brings a touch of flame to the Argyll hillside in early summer. In the foreground of the main picture *Embothrium coccineum*.

Inset left: *Crinodendron hookerianum*.

Inset right: *Desfontainia spinosa*.

The Chilean Rainforest

You are in a different world by the time you get to the Chilean area of Benmore. In perhaps 20 minutes of fairly brisk walking you have come a long way from the straight lines and symmetry of the Redwood Avenue.

There are paths and bridges here too but they twist and turn in the wild landscape at the most westerly point of Benmore. Picture the scene 20 years from now and imagine you are climbing through Chilean rainforest towards mountain tops bristling with the spiky green parasols of tall monkey puzzle trees. Halfway up you pass a clearing in the forest fringed by myrtles and climbing plants. On an early summer day the fire bush brings touches of flame to the hillside. It looks, smells and feels unlike any other part of the Garden.

Of course it is not quite like that yet. But the Chilean fire bush (*Embothrium coccineum*) does indeed flower on the Benmore hillside in late May and June. And although it will be a few years before the monkey puzzles (*Araucaria araucana*) are tall enough to dominate the skyline, already the young trees are developing a character of their own. Along with a collection of

other Chilean plants – *Pilgerodendron*, *Fitzroya*, *Nothofagus*, *Drimys* – they give a glimpse of the mountains of Chile.

The view looked very different until 1995 when the steep slope was cleared of sitka spruce, birch and *Rhododendron ponticum*. Bare ground opened up new habitats – streams, rock faces, tree stumps, sheltered shade and open ground – for a wealth of seed collected from expeditions to Chile. The first young specimens were introduced to the Scottish hillside after seed-collecting expeditions that began in 1994. Now the collection forms an important part of the International

Conifer Conservation Programme and includes eight of the nine Chilean conifers (the ninth is proving to be a challenge as it is the first time in cultivation for *Lepidothamnus fonkii* – a bizarre creeping conifer now growing in the Edinburgh Nursery). Beneath the trees are spectacular shrubs, grasses and herbaceous plants growing for the first time outside their native habitat.

In the wild many of these plants are threatened by fire, logging and changing land use. Overgrazing, invasive species and the spread of human populations all combine to destroy ecosystems rich in plants

Protecting Chile's threatened plants

During the 1996 expedition to Chile, Garden staff gathered seed as flames engulfed the forest behind them.

The best place for threatened plants is a secure habitat on home ground. But as the wilderness disappears it becomes increasingly important to collect seed for cultivation in a safe place – in hope of returning plants to the wild when conditions are right.

Led by Co-ordinator of the International Conifer Conservation Programme Martin Gardner, RBGE staff are involved in international conservation work with a highly innovative hands-on approach. A three-year Darwin Initiative project trained young Chilean postgraduates to help landowners and logging companies manage a sustainable living. The project ended with the publication of *Threatened Plants of Central and South Chile*, a practical field guide to identifying, cultivating, conserving – and celebrating – some of Chile's most endangered plants.

and animals found nowhere else on earth. Natural disasters like the 2010 earthquake and tsunami can also cause devastating destruction for people, plants and wildlife.

Even in the protected environment of the Garden there can be problems. Young plants need a careful helping hand – native heathers, grasses and the alien *R. ponticum* are always trying to return to the hillside. Chilean plants thrive on heavy rain and can stand up to cold winds but they long for more sunshine. The first fire bushes from seed collected on the Chilean island of Chiloé grew too fast and blew over. New seed collected in 2008 from cold, exposed summits of southern Chile has produced hardier plants now doing well at Benmore. In time maturing trees will create their own microclimate, sheltering young myrtles and overshadowing competition.

Expeditions produce more than wild seed. The memory of plants growing in their natural environment stays in the mind's eye of the collector and gardener. Curator Peter Baxter planted young *Pilgerodendron* trees in a straight row on the lower slopes of the Benmore hillside because that is how he saw the conifers growing in their native habitat as a result of seeding on fallen 'nurse' logs in a Chilean rainforest.

Top: Monkey puzzles (*Araucaria araucana*) in Chile's coastal mountain range in Parque Nacional Nahuelbuta, Chile.
Below: Mature monkey puzzles in the Sierra Nevada sector of Parque Nacional Conguillío, Chile.

Left: Benmore Curator Peter Baxter with RBGE's David Knott and Japanese botanist Matsushita Hirotaka on expedition in the Mount Daisen region of Japan (**main**).

Right: Pressing and photographing plants are part of a day's work in the field.

The Japanese Valley

In recent years, RBGE has been working in partnership with Japanese botanists on a series of major expeditions to Japan. These expeditions helped to build relationships and exchange expertise, and provided the wild seed to create the new plantings in the Japanese Valley.

To recreate a Japanese mountainside, a site was chosen in the Massan Valley. A glade of Japanese cedars (*Cryptomeria japonica*) had been planted here in the 1970s and were well-established trees by 2005. Over two winters, Benmore's horticulturists cleared the steep slopes of *Rhododendron ponticum* and sitka spruce. Then hundreds of Japanese trees and shrubs were planted on the precariously steep slopes, many surrounded by wire cages to protect them from grazing deer. The plantings are still young and small, but exploring here gives a taste of the future promise. Young maples, including *Acer rufinerve* and *A. capillipes*, now just delicate, red-branched saplings, will one day bring glorious autumn colour to this area of the garden. Still spindly birches will become elegant trees with shining, peeling bark, including *Betula maximowicziana*, one of the largest-leaved birches.

In clearing and planting the valley, as many as possible of the older trees were left standing, not just the Japanese cedars but also stands of Douglas fir, Noble fir and Caucasian fir higher up the slopes. The regional areas in the Garden are not rigidly defined – native heathers will spread beneath new introductions, and some plants will remain from an area's earlier incarnation: a beautiful old tree is not going to be removed just because the area has been relabelled. Likewise there are plenty of Japanese plants elsewhere in the Garden, including umbrella pines, day lilies and camellias.

The wild beauty of Benmore is a natural-looking landscape, evoking an impression of mountain habitats studded with rhododendrons. The Japanese rhododendrons here just add another dimension to this Benmore speciality. Soon Japanese ferns will cascade down the slope to meet those growing up from the Fernery.

26 September 2006 – Mount Daisen, Japan

We set out through the lowlands, walking through plantation forests of Japanese cypress, with maples just starting to show their autumn colour. We've had some pretty wet weather so it's a joy to see dappled foliage today, and the sun glinting through the trunks.

The vegetation changes as you gain height and we move into more natural woodland. Here there are magnolias and Japanese beech and Sasa – a sprawling, large-leaved bamboo. It's a gradual climb and we make our way in single file, taking notes and photos, collecting seed and making herbarium specimens.

It gets cooler as we get higher, into rowans and more maples, including Acer shirasawanum, with hints of gold and dark red. Many plants are familiar from RBGE's collections. It's interesting to see Shortia in abundance, which has often proved difficult to grow back in the Alpine Yard in Edinburgh, but here it is part of the thick ground cover, and beginning to turn deep purple.

A curtain of cloud has been draped along one side of the ridge all day, but the other side is clear and we look back beyond the spine of the mountain to the lowlands and ahead to the rocky summit overlooking Mount Daisen. The vegetation is thicker here and we scramble through, noting the viburnum, the red rowan berries and gnarled old Japanese yews.

It gets dark early, and very quickly here, there isn't the same lengthy twilight that we have back home, so we have to make our way down before 6.00. It's been a magical day.

David Knott

The change in atmosphere and temperature enhances the sensation of entering another world – an enchanted world where an ancient family of plants flourishes. Ferns are everywhere: sprouting from the rocks in delicate feathery fountains, creeping along the ground and cascading down the walls. Tree ferns tower above, broad fronds reaching up to the high vaulted roof.

The Fernery dates back to a time when Britain was gripped by fern-mania. Throughout the country, people were collecting and exchanging ferns, admiring their varieties, debating their classification and even decorating all manner of household artefacts with images of ferns. Exploring here, it's easy to understand what so fascinated the Victorians: ferns are intricate, beautiful and astonishingly diverse.

It must have been a costly undertaking to build and maintain a heated fernery so far up the rocky hillside, but at the time there was no better way to display your wealth, status and fashionable taste than to dazzle your guests with a lush and

The Benmore Fernery

Deep in the Garden and high on the hillside, a winding path climbs a steep slope to the newly restored Benmore Fernery. Amidst rocky cliffs, stepping through the small doorway feels like entering a cave, but stone steps lead up to a dazzle of light and space and lush greenery.

Clockwise from left: Stone steps lead from the entrance vault into the light of the Fernery; a young frond, or 'fiddlehead', unfurls; the newly restored building; some of the 70 fern species represented; the restoration meant heavy work in steep slopes; just the skeleton of walls and roof remained on the ruined building.

exotic collection of ferns. James Duncan, then owner of the estate, constructed the Fernery in the 1870s, an additional flourish to delight his guests who travelled from far and wide to admire his extensive art collection.

By 1889, Duncan's fortunes had turned; he sold the estate and through time the Fernery fell into disrepair. By 1929, when Benmore was gifted to RBGE, it was in a dilapidated state with only its walls and roof structure remaining. Without heat and care, the original showcase collection of ferns had long since gone, though native species had moved in and claimed the derelict building, colonising the damp and shady ground inside and around it.

Benmore's Curators, the Younger (Benmore) Trustees and the Friends of the Garden longed to restore the Fernery to its former glory, but for many years this seemed an implausible dream. Then, in 1992, the Fernery was designated as a listed building by Historic Scotland, which proved a catalyst to explore whether the dream could be realised. The project gained momentum with the support of the Younger (Benmore) Trust, the Heritage Lottery Fund and a very successful appeal to RBGE Members. Reconstruction work began in 2008 – repairing the walls, recreating the paths and replacing the roof. Over

the summer of 2009, the building and surrounding area was landscaped and planted – filled with ferns ready for the formal opening in September 2009.

A part of Benmore's history has been brought back to life – but the Fernery is also a contemporary story, exploring the place of these ancient plants in the world of today. RBGE is a world leader in fern conservation and most plants here have been grown from spores and are of known wild origin from expeditions throughout the world. The Fernery enables visitors to learn about their history and life cycles, and above all to admire their intricate and diverse beauty – highlighting a group of plants that are so often in the shade.

Native Woodland Area

In the shadow of giant conifers and towering rhododendrons, it is easy to overlook the beauty of smaller, less conspicuous plant groups like the mosses and liverworts, lichens, ferns and fungi. But a change in focus reveals how much these plants contribute to Benmore's character.

Though small, these plants play the largest part in connecting the landscape. They transform the Garden into an enchanted woodland, draping the steep hillside in a soft, green blanket and soothing the hard edges of rock and bark. Look down and you'll see that the woodland floor is strewn with springy cushions made of miniature stars. Look up – the highest branches of the broadleaves are sprouting ferns and festooned with lichens; even the tiniest twigs are wrapped in green velvet.

Mosses, ferns and lichens anchor the lower branches of the conifers to the ground. They hold these exotic historic collections to their new home on Scotland's western edge. North American spruces and Himalayan birches alike are claimed by native bryophytes (mosses and liverworts); wherever they come from, new arrivals from around the world are soon colonised and decorated so they look at home in Scotland's own rainforest.

Left and below: Mosses, lichens and ferns unify the Benmore landscape, colonising the banks of streams and forming new habitats on fallen trees (**above right**).
Insets from top: Mosses *Hypnum andoi* and *Dicranum scoparium*, and the fungi turkey tail (*Trametes versicolor*).

These plants flourish at Benmore because of its location in the oceanic habitat of Argyll. Close by are remnants of ancient forests which once cloaked much of the Highlands and stretched along the western seaboard of Britain and Ireland. These Atlantic woodlands are dominated by oak and birch and host an abundance of ferns, mosses, liverworts and lichens, which luxuriate in the mild climate, regular rainfall and the shelter and humidity provided by the tree canopy.

Scotland's remaining Atlantic woodlands are now the richest habitat in Europe for bryophytes and are home to many rare lichens, some of which occur nowhere else in the world. This gives the woodlands an important international significance, and gives Scotland a special responsibility to look after them.

The Native Woodland Area was created at Benmore to celebrate this status, and to draw attention to these smaller stars of Scotland's flora. A sheltered area was cleared of larch and rhododendrons to make way for the planting of native trees. The site is a natural outdoor classroom, with

a rocky cliff face and tumbling burn providing a perfect setting for mosses and liverworts. Bryophyte gardening is mostly a question of getting the conditions right – with enough shelter, shade and humidity, these delicate, moisture-loving species will arrive by themselves.

It all looks so natural you could think nothing is happening here and walk on by. But this is an experiment in recreating a dynamic habitat every bit as bold as the plantings of Japan or Tasmania. So much is happening here, but it's a drama on a different scale. Slowly, silently, lower plants are colonising the site – spreading over the ground, flourishing beside the burn, nestling into every schism in the craggy rock. Fallen logs and stumps are engulfed and transformed into intimate landscapes, sprouting ferns and fungi. The exposed cliff face is decorated with an intricate tapestry of colours and textures – pale grey coral-like curls of lichen, splashes of soft ochre, smudges of white and olive, soft mounds of russet and brilliant green.

To see it, you just have to stop and look closer.

A nearly natural history of Benmore

A flash of red in the green, a flickering of wings over water, the hoot of an owl at dusk – a walk at Benmore can bring close encounters with a teeming, jostling community of wildlife: prey and predators, pollinators and pests, all thriving in the shelter of the Garden.

It wasn't always a safe place to be a bird or a beast. In the winter of 1893 the Younger Game Book recorded a culling of 37 cats, 16 foxes and 3 hedgehogs along with ravens, rabbits, jackdaws, jays, magpies, hawks, weasels and squirrels. They were the vermin eliminated to protect the game. After that, pheasants were reared by the thousand on the estate. Red grouse, woodcock, black grouse and capercaillie also went into the game bag.

Some things change. Pheasants are no longer bred at Benmore, deer and rabbits are still pests (though these days rabbit numbers fluctuate with epidemics of myxomatosis). But black grouse and red squirrel are now on the red list of the Argyll and Bute Local Biodiversity Action Plan. The list of threatened or declining species includes birds which used to be regarded as common or garden – cuckoos, fieldfares, hen harriers, redwings and spotted flycatchers.

You won't find all of them in the Garden. But like all sensitively managed gardens the cultivated environment

Left: A native red squirrel arrives to seek food and shelter among the conifers.

Above: A tree creeper on redwood bark.

Facing page, clockwise from top left: A greater spotted woodpecker finds easy pickings in the peanut feeder; a young male siskin keeps a watchful eye; frogs spawning.

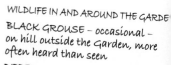

of Benmore is an important sanctuary for wildlife – the sheer size and diversity of woodland plantings offers a wonderful mosaic of habitats.

Spotted flycatchers find nesting places in climbers on walls of the Formal Garden. Treecreepers snuggle into the soft bark of giant redwoods. Hedgehogs enjoy rich pickings around rotting conifers. Daubenton's bats swoop over the river. Even otters have been spotted by the stream in the Chilean Glade. Moss-covered trees and plants from all over the world are food and shelter to native insects, birds and animals.

Red squirrels enjoy Benmore's mixed conifers and broadleaved trees of different ages. Rarely seen in Britain outside Scotland and Northern England, red squirrels are common across the forested landscape of Argyll. But, being on the list of globally threatened species, they are still carefully monitored in the Cowal area.

Apart from the threat of grey squirrels (they spread disease as well as competing for food) the red's biggest danger is road traffic. Now Benmore also offers red squirrels a safe feeding place far from the main road. If you take a walk in the Eachaig Arboretum (turn right through the gate in the deer fence) you might just catch sight of that tingling red flash in the green wood.

WILDLIFE IN AND AROUND THE GARDEN

BLACK GROUSE – occasional – on hill outside the Garden, more often heard than seen

DIPPER – common – nest every year below footbridge and vehicle bridge over River Eachaig

GOLDEN EAGLE – occasional – seen circling high above the Garden

MISTLE THRUSH – common – resident breeding population swelled by large numbers of autumn migrants

SPARROWHAWK – frequent – seen taking greenfinches in Formal Garden

TAWNY OWL – common – mainly heard at night. Numbers thought to be healthy. Nest boxes in the Garden and neighbouring woodland

TREECREEPER – very common – carve out depressions in soft bark of giant redwoods to shelter from the elements

WILLOW WARBLER – common – the sound of spring and summer

MINK – occasional – used to be frequent at the Pond when it was stocked with carp

OTTER – rare? – being quite secretive they may be more common than supposed. Seen a few years ago in the Chilean Glade area. In this area of Cowal sightings are becoming much more frequent

RED SQUIRREL – common – two feeding boxes recently installed with a view to erecting a hide to enable visitors to have more frequent sightings

WEASEL – occasional – probably common but not often seen due to their secretive nature

WILDCAT – occasional – rarely seen. An animal with a radio collar was released in the area a few years ago

Above: An extract of notes made over the winter of 2009-10 by Neil McCheyne, Benmore Garden Supervisor, for the RBGE Biodiversity Action Group.

Education, exhibitions, events
Inspired by the Garden

With green face paint dripping in the rain, local schoolchildren run down the hill laughing, returning to the Courtyard Gallery from a Celtic trail around the Garden, where they met a druid and learnt the folklore of native plants.

The children are here for the annual Schools Week, which brings RBGE's Edinburgh-based education team to Benmore each September to offer events for children and their teachers from schools in the surrounding area. Often the same schools return each year, so the team ensure there is always a new theme, linking exploration with an arts activity.

One year the children got acquainted with plant classification through the 'Green Kingdom' event, learning through printing with ferns and leaves. Another year the focus was China – an expedition with compass, map and base camp for the older pupils, while the younger ones discovered a suitable habitat for a panda bears' picnic.

Benmore is much more than a Garden; it has become a hub – a place where people can gather to engage with the plant kingdom and with each other. The picturesque Gallery with its cobbled courtyard now hosts a diverse range of activities for all ages throughout the year. Regular exhibitions showcase the wider work of RBGE or highlight interpretations

Clockwise from left: Drawing inspiration from the Garden in the majestic Redwood Avenue; local schoolchildren meet a Celtic druid during Benmore's Schools Week; artwork created during a course at the Garden; the Courtyard Gallery is a focus for arts and activities.

of the natural world through art, photography and crafts.

Like many of the world's leading botanic gardens, RBGE has evolved in recent years from a scientific institution focused on the study of plantlife to a multi-faceted organisation with an ever-increasing focus on public engagement. Botanic gardens of the 21st century have something new to say, a message of vital importance to the world today — that plants are the basis of all life on Earth, and that if people are to survive we must learn to understand and appreciate the plants that sustain the complex ecosystem we belong to.

Spreading that message can take many forms – a vibrant education programme to stimulate enjoyment and interest in the natural world, arts activities to encourage closer observation and deeper engagement,

talks, lectures and horticultural training to share skills and expertise. Above all botanic gardens offer a place for people to come and marvel at the beauty and diversity of plants, to feel a sense of wonder, and a platform to further discuss, debate and explore.

Whether walking slowly through the Redwood Avenue, looking at a rhododendron leaf through a microscope or admiring a photo in a Gallery exhibition, Benmore invites you in to be inspired.

RBGE Members

The Garden is a much-loved resource for the local community and many activities at Benmore are run by the vibrant group of RBGE Members. They offer a lively programme of activities – growing plants for the popular annual plant sale, visiting other gardens and inviting RBGE specialists to share their tales of exploration and discovery through a series of afternoon lectures. Some Members also act as Garden Guides, offering tours to visitors and sharing their knowledge of and enthusiasm for Benmore.

Above: Painting by Pamela Richardson.

Seasonal highlights in the Garden

In summer you might be tempted to go no further than the Pond, where Himalayan poppies, rhododendrons, rodgersias, hostas, veratrums and ornamental grasses reflect colours and textures in the water – but it would be a shame not to see the Chilean fire bush flaming on the hillside at the far western corner of the Garden.

In winter you might linger beneath giant redwoods, warm to the touch and reaching higher into the sky than the pale sun – but it is worth wandering further to find surprisingly bright green mosses carpeting the ground in Glen Massan. Or even just to see the different silhouettes of trees set against a bright winter sky.

In short, it is worth exploring deeper into the Garden at any time of year. Each season brings surprises of changing light, colour and fragrance to tempt you further in and higher up the slopes. Whichever route you take you will find something new, whether it is wrapped in mist, etched against snow, lapping up sun or sparkling through raindrops.

Main: Around James Duncan's bronze fountain, Boy with Two Dolphins, Benmore Pond reflects changing colours of the seasons.
Inset right: Fiery orange *Rhododendron* 'Norma'.

Spring

Rhododendrons are already celebrating the end of winter by the time the Garden officially opens for a new season on 1 March. A sudden frost can turn the blossom brown but more often than not spring brings a surprising burst of warm colours to the hillside: fiery scarlets and sizzling pinks joining the splash of yellow narcissus beneath trees and shrubs.

Colour is not just for blossom. On the lower slopes of A'Chruach, *Rhododendron barbatum* produces plum-coloured flaking bark and *R. thomsonii* a striking gold and sea-green peeling bark as well as vivid red flowers. On sunny days, magnolias are spectacular pink and white against blue sky between the Viewpoint and Golden Gates Avenue. And there are sweet smells in the air from *Osmanthus delavayi* in April and *Pieris japonica* in May.

Young shoots bring sharp freshness to evergreens. Deciduous larches produce a flush of grass-green leaves. Perhaps most spectacular of all, the myrtle beech, *Nothofagus cunninghamii*, is quietly producing a shock of brilliant new leaves of red and bronze on the Tasmanian Ridge.

Above left: Spring fever from *Nothofagus cunninghamii*.
Above right: A young robin ventures out.
Below: A troop of narcissi brave a late fall of snow beneath the giant redwoods.

Summer

Late-flowering rhododendrons and azaleas blend spring into early summer at Benmore. Deep red Chilean lantern bushes also carry the flame of spring's rich and riotous colour. Then a wave of white flowers arrives, delicate and sweetly scented, shining against the brilliant greens of the summer garden: tiny, pink-tinged bells of enkianthas, fragrant, white droplets of Japanese snowbells (*Styrax japonica*) and elegant, downward-facing flowers on the luxurious, summer-flowering *Magnolia wilsonii*.

In July and August, the Japanese shrub *Clethra barbinervis* is covered in long strands of fragrant white flowers, to the delight of butterflies and bees, as well as visitors to the Garden.

Eucryphias, or leatherwoods, from the temperate rainforests of the southern hemisphere, thrive in Argyll's warm, wet climate and are a speciality at Benmore, their pure white flowers against glossy leaves bringing a spring-like freshness into August and September.

Clockwise from top: A dazzle of colour from *Primula* and rhododendrons; blue poppies *Meconopsis grandis* bring a spark of summer skies beside the pond; the delicate blooms of *Magnolia wilsonii*; and *Styrax japonica*.

Autumn

Autumn burns brightly in Benmore. Enkianthus are now vibrant in yellow and scarlet foliage, rowans and cotoneasters are crowded with berries and deciduous azaleas turn glorious hues of red and orange.

The heart of the blaze is around the Pond. Fire meets water where the flaming colours of the Japanese maples are reflected on the still surface. The apricot-tinged yellow leaves of the katsura tree smell of caramel – an unforgettable treat in autumn is to stand beneath this tree as leaves fall into the Pond. Whichever way you look, the colours dazzle against a rich backdrop of conifers, whether the soft green spires of the redwoods or the bluish hue of the plantations on the mountains.

The colour continues throughout the Garden and throughout the season. Behind Benmore House, the Persian ironwood (*Parrotia persica*) celebrates every autumn shade, with glossy purples, brilliant reds, oranges and creamy yellows. On the Younger Memorial Walk, *Sorbus alnifolia* – the largest in Britain – holds its leaves well as they turn yellow and bronze. In the last days of October, autumn's embers are still glowing, the colours more subdued. Skeleton branches hold on to the last red berries. Conifers are defined against the soft gold of larches.

Main and right: Going out with a blaze, Maples reflect fire in the pond as the Garden closes for the season. But Members of RBGE can still enjoy a winter walk among the trees and the chance to see Puck's Hut covered in snow.

Left, above: Benmore's conifers in the autumn mist.

Below, from left: Seasonal colour from the whitebeam *Sorbus thibetica* and the paperbark maple *Acer griseum*.

Winter

During the short days of winter the Garden is officially closed to visitors as staff prepare for the new season, but restricted access may be possible by contacting the Curator.

There is a magical quality to northern light which picks up the subtleties of a woodland at rest: the deeply fissured bark of Douglas fir with its almost prehistoric, dinosaur-skin look about it; the startling white of Himalayan birch (*Betula utilis* var. *jacquemontii*), and almost everywhere the profusion of mosses, lichens and liverworts covering the ground with green, pink-red and rusty brown.

Sometimes (as in the long, hard winter of 2009–10) a sharp cold spell brings a different look to the Garden with giant redwoods standing out redder than ever against the snow.

Red, pink and white berries on rowans and whitebeams often last well into December. And by February *Rhododendron barbatum* is already eager for spring again.

Royal
Botanic Garden
Edinburgh

ISBN 978-1-906129-72-9
Benmore Botanic Garden Guidebook

Supported by

The Royal Botanic Garden Edinburgh is a Charity registered in Scotland (number SC007983)
and is supported by the Scottish Government Rural and Environmental Research and Analysis Directorate.

Written by

Anna Levin and Fay Young

Designed by

Caroline Muir, RBGE

Photography

Peter Baxter
Laurie Campbell
Peter Clarke
Cath Evans
Martin Gardner
Peter Hollingsworth
Vlasta Jamnický
David Knott
Loch Lomond & The Trossachs National Park Authority
David Long
Neil McCheyne
Robert Unwin
Andrew Watson
Debbie White
Lynsey Wilson

Published by

Royal Botanic Garden Edinburgh
20A Inverleith Row
Edinburgh EH3 5LR
United Kingdom

Printed by

Potts Print (UK), Northumberland

Mixed Sources
Product group from well-managed
forests and other controlled sources
www.fsc.org Cert no. TT-COC-002184
© 1996 Forest Stewardship Council